Non-fiction 5

Series Editor: Pie Corbett

CAMBRIDGE
UNIVERSITY PRESS

CAMBRIDGE UNIVERSITY PRESS
Cambridge, New York, Melbourne, Madrid, Cape Town, Singapore, São Paulo

Cambridge University Press
The Edinburgh Building, Cambridge CB2 2RU, UK

www.cambridge.org
Information on this title: www.cambridge.org/9780521618885

First published 2006

Printed in the United Kingdom at the University Press, Cambridge

A catalogue record for this publication is available from the British Library

ISBN-13 978-0-521-61888-5 paperback
ISBN-10 0-521-61888-6 paperback

ACKNOWLEDGEMENTS

Cover
Lee Foster

Photos
p.27, p.32 Donald C. & Priscilla Alexander Eastman; p.29 John Elk III;
p.33 Anders Blomqvist; p.35 Jean Paul Ferrero; p.36 Masahiro Lijima;
p.37 John Cancalosi; p.38, p.39 D. Parer & E. Parer Cook; p.40 Mitchell
Library, State Library of New South Wales; p.41 Australian Koala Foundation,
www.savethekoala.com, Joan Limon, Jo Knights, Renee Sternberg; p.45,
p.47, p.48 Action Plus; p.53 Digital Vision / Getty Images

Artwork
Beehive Illustration (Robin Edwards, Peter Richardson), HL Studios

Texts
Recounts: Texts by Ruth Thompson
Non-chronological reports: Texts by Teresa Saunders
Persuasive writing: Texts by Gill Matthews

Contents

Recounts

The Disastrous Expedition of Burke and Wills

Part One

In 1860, no European had ever ventured across central Australia from south to north – a distance of nearly 2,400 miles.

On 18 August 1860, thousands of well-wishers gathered in Melbourne's Royal Park. They had come to see Robert Burke and his men set off on this trek across Australia, from Melbourne to the Gulf of Carpentaria. Burke, once a police inspector, had been chosen by the state of Victoria to lead the expedition. He hoped to claim the £2,000 prize offered by the Australian government for finding a south–north route across the continent.

The expedition set off with twenty-five camels, brought specially from India, and two dozen packhorses. Burke rode a dappled grey horse, called Billy. Wagons carried tents,

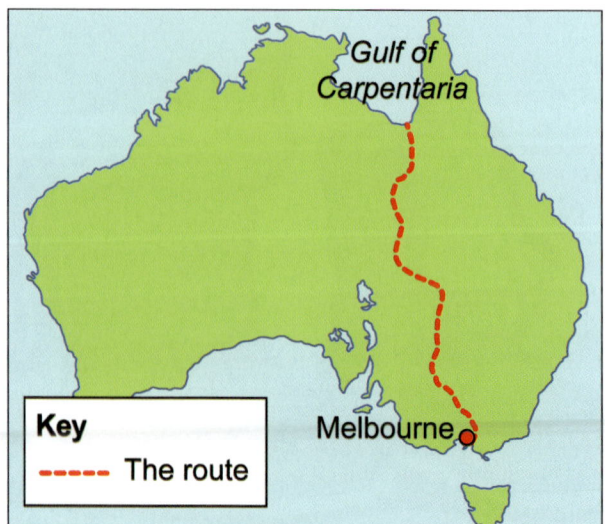

Key
----- The route

guns, rockets, camp beds, tools and scientific equipment, as well as two years' supply of food, including dried meat, flour, oatmeal, sugar, rice and rum. The explorers had also taken lime juice, preserved vegetables and dried fruit to prevent scurvy. They had packed beads and mirrors as gifts for the Aboriginals.

They had not gone far when several wagons broke down on the rough ground. Burke realised that they were overloaded, and dumped some of the supplies. Soon after, he argued fiercely with his second-in-command, Landells. The problem was the camels. Landells was in charge of them and, in Burke's opinion, pampered the animals. Burke wanted them to carry more weight. Landells said his interference was "a stretch of despotic power not to be endured for a moment". Then there was the

problem of the rum. Landells gave it to the camels to revive them when necessary. Unfortunately, the men decided to drink it as well. Burke was furious to have drunken men on his hands and demanded the rum be left behind. This was too much for Landells, who resigned. Burke promoted William Wills, a surveyor, in his place.

When they reached Menindie, the last settlement, Burke split his party, so he could travel more quickly. He chose eight companions and left William Wright, an experienced guide, in charge of the supplies, telling him to follow on. Each night, the advance party blazed a tree with the letter B and the number of their camp, so that Wright and the other men could find them.

Part Two

On 11 November, Burke and his men reached Cooper's Creek. They set up camp LXV (their sixty-fifth) to wait for Wright and the others. After six weeks, they had still not arrived, so Burke impatiently decided to make for the Gulf of Carpentaria. He knew that another explorer, John McDouall Stuart, was also attempting to cross the continent and Burke was determined to beat him, even if the newspaper did not think he could.

Burke picked Wills, a seaman named Charlie Gray and a young ex-solider called John King to go with him. They chose six camels to carry three months' stores, and Burke took Billy, his horse. Burke instructed the men left behind, under the command of William Brahe, to build a wooden fort and to wait for as long as possible for their return.

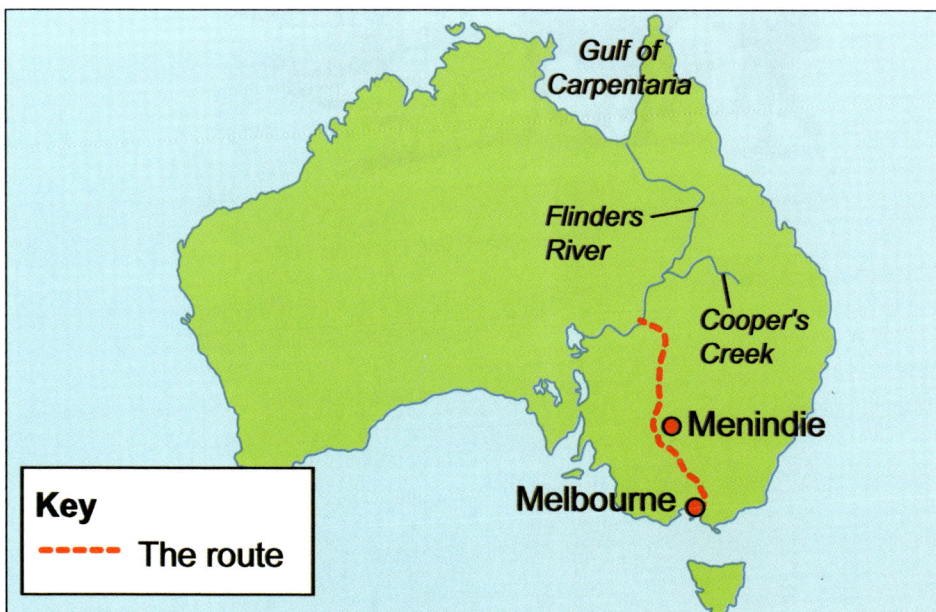

Key

----- The route

Burke and his men trekked north. It was hot and dry, but they found plenty of fresh water to drink, fish and ducks to eat, and grass for their animals on the way. Eventually, they came to the Flinders River. The surrounding country was too swampy for camels, so Burke and Wills set off on foot to the coast. They came to a salty, tidal channel and knew that the sea could not be far off but, without a boat, there was no way to reach it.

It was time to turn back. Their journey had already taken almost two months and they had eaten more than two-thirds of their stores. They had to get back to Cooper's Creek before their food ran out and also before Brahe left for Menindie.

Part Three

The return was awful. There were constant storms and the hot, humid air and slippery, slimy mud made the going slow. Burke reduced rations to a little flour and meat for each man, so they soon became weak as well as hungry. Charlie Gray stole extra rations of flour and Burke gave him a thrashing. With 500 kilometres still to go, their supplies were almost gone, so they shot three camels and Burke's horse for meat. Gray became so weak and ill that he had to be tied to his camel. On 16 April he died. His companions buried him, but were so exhausted by the effort, that they had to wait a day before moving on.

Finally, on 21 April 1861, Burke, Wills and King arrived at the depot at Cooper's Creek. It was deserted, but there was a message cut into a tree, which read:

DIG

3FT N.W.

APR 21 1861

They dug as they were told and found supplies and a note from Brahe, who wrote that he had left that very morning for Menindie. Burke thought of trying to catch up with him, but the three of them were too weak, their legs almost paralysed and their camels too exhausted. Instead, they decided to follow Cooper's Creek and then head for the nearest outpost. Before they left, Burke and Wills buried a message describing their plans under the tree, just in case rescuers showed up. However, they did not blaze a new mark to show what they had done. This proved a fatal mistake.

Key

----- The route
----- The return

Gulf of Carpentaria

Flinders River

Cooper's Creek

Menindie

Melbourne

Part Four

Still weak, the three men slowly followed the creek. Within a week, disaster struck. One of the camels got bogged down in quicksand. Soon after, the other two collapsed and died, even though they had thrown away supplies to lighten the animals' loads. Luckily, the men met some Aboriginals, who gave them fish and cakes of nardoo.

In the meantime, Brahe and Wright had met up. They decided to ride together to camp LXV for a last look, just in case Burke had turned up. However, everything seemed just as they had left it. Nothing new had been carved on the tree and the ground beneath seemed undisturbed – so they rode away again.

Burke and his men made a last attempt to reach the outpost. After trekking

across sand and cracked earth, with no water to be found, they realised it was hopeless and returned to Cooper's Creek. They ate the nardoo, but slowly grew weaker and weaker. Soon Wills could no longer stand up. Burke and King left him to go in search of help from Aboriginals, but Burke collapsed and died on the way.

King pressed on for a few days and managed to shoot some birds. He took these back to Wills, only to find that he, too, had died. Fortunately, King found some friendly Aboriginals who looked after him for two months until a rescue party found him. He alone had survived to tell the tale of the tragic expedition.

Scott's South Pole Diary

Part One

In the early 20th century, no one had ever reached the South Pole. Two explorers, Robert Scott, from Britain, and Roald Amundsen, a Norwegian, were both determined to be the first to get there.

On 26 November 1910, Robert Falcon Scott and his party set out from Port Lyttleton, New Zealand, aboard the ship *Terra Nova*. They set up expedition headquarters at Cape Evans and started their actual journey towards the South Pole on Tuesday 24 October 1911. They set off with sledges hauled by motors, ponies and dogs – but in the end they pulled the sledges themselves. These extracts from Scott's diary tell the story of his journey.

Friday, November 3, 1911

Our ponies marched steadily and well together over the sea ice.

Saturday, November 4

Some 4 miles out we met a tin pathetically inscribed "Big end Day's motor No.2 cylinder broken". Half a mile beyond, we found the motor ... the dream of great help from the machines is at an end.

Tuesday, November 7

A blizzard has continued throughout last night and late in the afternoon ... The ponies were distressed as usual when the snow began to fall ... it is satisfactory to find dogs will pull the loads and can be driven to face such a wind as we have had.

Luckily, the blizzard did not last long.

Thursday, November 9

Sticking to programme ... things look hopeful. The weather is beautiful – temp +12, with a bright sun.

Sunday, November 12

Our marches are uniformly horrid just at present ... The weather was horrid, overcast, gloomy, snowy. One's spirits became very low.

Wednesday, November 22

Everything much the same. The ponies thinner but not much weaker ... The dogs are in good form still and came up well with their loads ... The weather is glorious.

Several days later, everything changed.

Tuesday, November 28

The most dismal start imaginable. Thick as a hedge, snow falling and

drifting with keen southerly wind...

Tuesday, December 5

We awoke this morning to a raging, howling blizzard...

Part Two

Bad weather lasted for several more days. Food ran short – both for the men and the animals – and Scott was worried.

Saturday, December 9

... the weather slowly improving. The tremendous snowfall ... had made the surface intolerably soft ... At 8 p.m. the ponies were quite done ... We camped and the ponies have been shot. Poor beasts!

Wednesday, December 13

A most dismal day ... we have advanced a bare 4 miles today ... Our height is now about 1,500 feet.

Monday, January 1

We have been rising again all day ... The temperature is steadily falling ... We are very comfortable in our double tent. Stick of chocolate to celebrate the New Year.

Thursday, January 11

About 74 miles from the Pole – can we keep this up for seven days? None of us ever had such hard work before.

They *did* keep it up, however – even though the temperature was 25 degrees below zero Fahrenheit [–32 degrees Celsius]. Soon, they were full of hope.

Night, January 15

It is wonderful to see that two long marches will land us at the Pole.

Tuesday, January 16

Bowers detected a black speck ahead. We marched on, found it was a black flag … nearby the remains of a camp; sledge tracks coming and going and the clear trace of dogs' paws. This told us the whole story. The Norwegians … are the first to the Pole. It is a terrible disappointment to me…

Wednesday, January 17

The Pole. Yes, but under very different circumstances from those expected … Great God! This is an awful place … Well, it is something to have got here…

Thursday morning, January 18

We have just arrived at this tent … we find a record of five Norwegians having been here. A note from Amundsen … asks me to forward a letter to King Haakon … We built a cairn, put up our poor slighted Union Jack, and photographed ourselves.

The party rested and reflected upon their bad luck.

Part Three

After discovering that they had arrived too late, Scott's party turned around. The journey across the ice and snow had taken 2 months 17 days, so a similar long trek faced them on the way back.

Monday, January 22

We marched a solid 9 hours, and thus we have covered 14.5 miles but it has been a grind. We are within … 30 miles from our depot and with 5 days' food in hand.

Tuesday, January 23

The old tracks show so remarkably well that we can follow them without much difficulty … We came along at a great rate and should have got within easy reach of our depot had not Wilson suddenly discovered that Evans' nose was frostbitten – it was white and hard.

Two days later, there were more problems.

Thursday, January 25

Thank God we found our Half Degree depot … Only 89 miles to the next depot, but it is time we cleared off

this plateau … Oates suffers from a cold foot; Evans' eye and nose are in a bad state, and tonight Wilson is suffering tortures from his eye...

Tuesday, January 30

We have passed the last cairn before the depot, the track is clear ahead, the weather fair, the wind helpful, the gradient down...

The men trudged on for two weeks.

Wednesday, February 14

… we are not pulling strong: probably none of us … the worst case is Evans … This morning he suddenly disclosed a huge blister on his foot.

Friday, February 16

A rather trying position. Evans has nearly broken down in brain, we think...

Saturday, February 17

A very terrible day. Evans started in his place … but had to leave the sledge … later he dropped out again … We had to push on … After lunch and Evans still not appearing … all four started back on ski. I was first to reach the poor man … he showed every sign of complete collapse. Bowers and I went back for the sledge … when we returned he was practically unconscious. He died quietly at 12.30 a.m.

Part Four

Nearly three weeks after Evans' death, there was worse to come.

<u>Monday, March 5</u>

Regret to say going from bad to worse. Oates' feet are in a wretched condition. One swelled up tremendously last night and he is very lame this morning…

<u>Saturday, March 10</u>

Things steadily downhill. Oates' foot worse.

<u>Friday, March 16, or Saturday 17</u>

Tragedy all along the line … poor Titus Oates said he couldn't go on … He slept through the night before last, hoping not to wake; but he woke in the morning. It was blowing a blizzard. He said, "I am just going outside and may be some time." He went out into the blizzard and we have not seen him since.

The men knew that they had to go on.

March 19

Today we started in the usual dragging manner. Sledge dreadfully heavy … We have two days' food, but barely a day's fuel. All our feet are getting bad … The weather doesn't give us a chance: −40 temp. today.

Thursday, March 29

Since the 21st we have had a continuous gale. We had fuel to make two cups of tea apiece and bare food for two days. Every day we have been ready to start for our depot 11 miles away, but outside the door of the tent it remains a scene of whirling drift. I do not think we can hope for better things now. We shall stick it out to the end, but we are getting weaker, of course, and the end cannot be far. It seems a pity, but I cannot write more −

For God's sake look after our people.

R Scott

Extracts from Scott's Diaries

Wednesday, November 22

Everything much the same. The ponies thinner but not much weaker ... The dogs are in good form still and came up well with their loads ... The weather is glorious.

Monday, January 1

We have been rising again all day ... The temperature is steadily falling ... We are very comfortable in our double tent. Stick of chocolate to celebrate the New Year.

Tuesday, January 16

Bowers detected a black speck ahead. We marched on, found it was a black flag … nearby the remains of a camp; sledge tracks coming and going and the clear trace of dogs' paws. This told us the whole story. The Norwegians … are the first to the Pole. It is a terrible disappointment to me…

Saturday, February 17

A very terrible day. Evans started in his place … but had to leave the sledge … later he dropped out again … We had to push on … After lunch and Evans still not appearing … all four started back on ski. I was first to reach the poor man … he showed every sign of complete collapse. Bowers and I went back for the sledge … when we returned he was practically unconscious. He died quietly at 12.30 a.m.

Non-chronological reports

Travel Guide Book – Egypt

The visitor to Egypt will experience an endless stream of treasures – a countryside rich in contrasts, ancient tombs, religious sites and cities still bustling after thousands of years.

Land of Contrasts

Egypt is a land of contrasts: sometimes noisy and crowded, sometimes empty desert. Parts of it are green and fertile; mostly it is dry and arid. Warm breezes cool the northern seashores, while the ferocious khamsin whips up sandstorms out in the desert. On the edge of the Western Desert, the land plunges to 130 metres below sea level, but towards the east between the Nile and the Red Sea, mountain ranges reach up more than 2,000 metres. In spite of all its differences, Egypt is always hot, dusty and endlessly fascinating.

Five thousand years ago, the country created one of the world's greatest ancient civilisations. Egypt's magnificent monuments and priceless treasures are still telling its story today. Wherever you go, from the bustling capital of Cairo to the peaceful southern town of Aswan, there are reminders of Egypt's historic past.

Ancient Egyptians believed that their country was the centre of the world – if you look at a map of the earth's land mass, you will see that they were right. The Ancient Egyptians worked out that the Great Pyramid at Giza is at the centre of the planet's land mass.

The Ancient Egyptians also believed that the gods favoured them above everyone else and gave them the gift of the Nile. Egypt's whole geography and development is shaped by the river; everything, both past and present, follows its course. Along its banks, sacred cities grew, pharaohs were buried and temples and shrines were built to give thanks to the gods for their generosity.

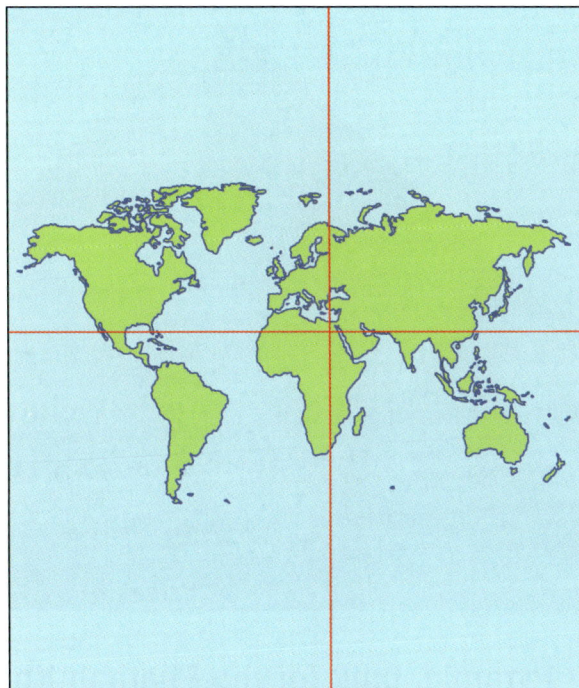

Egypt at the centre of the world

Pyramids and the Sphinx

The pyramids at Giza are one of the world's most visited ancient sites and are a perfect introduction to Ancient Egypt. It is best to arrive early in the morning or towards sunset to experience the true splendour of these three mighty tombs. The pyramids, which tower towards the sky, were built as burial chambers for the pharaohs Khufu, Khafra and Menkaura. They were made from blocks of carefully carved yellow limestone and their corners line up exactly with north, south, east and west. It is hard to imagine that they were built more than 4,500 years ago.

The Great Pyramid, built for the Pharaoh Khufu, is the last remaining Wonder of the Ancient World. Its sheer size and sense of history is breathtaking. Originally, it was thought that the pyramids were constructed by slaves, but archaeologists now think that they were built by willing farmers, who left their land to work at Giza during the time of the annual Nile floods.

Alongside the pyramids is the Sphinx, built by Pharaoh Khafra in his image to watch over his tomb. This enormous figure of a lion's body with a pharaoh's head is carved from a large outcrop of limestone and dates from 2,500 BC. Between the front paws of the Sphinx is a stele telling the story of Tuthmosis IV. According to legend, desert storms buried the Sphinx beneath the sand. Tuthmosis dreamt that, if he could uncover it, he would become pharaoh. He quickly set to work to clear away the sand – and his dream came true.

Tombs and Temples

Luxor is famed for its tombs and temples. For many centuries, it was the capital and spiritual centre of Ancient Egypt. The word "Luxor" comes from the Arab name "al-Uqsor", which means "the palaces".

The visitor will be drawn to a spectacular avenue of life-size sphinxes, each showing the head of a ram and the body of a lion. The avenue links the Temple of Luxor, in the heart of the town, to the great Temple of Amon three kilometres away at Karnak. It also highlights how important Luxor was as a religious centre.

Karnak was the largest temple site ever built by the Ancient Egyptians. For thirteen centuries, each new pharaoh added a new garden or obelisk or altar to mark his time as ruler. But nothing compares with the Great Hypostyle Hall, which was begun by Amenophis and finished many years later by Seti I

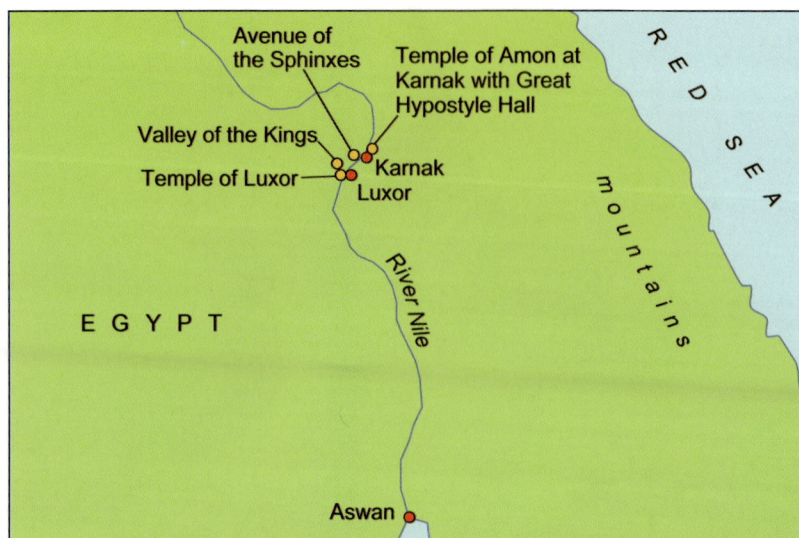

and his son Ramses. Entering the hall is like walking into a dense stone forest, with row upon row of enormous, spectacularly carved and decorated columns reaching up to the roof.

A thousand years after the pyramids were built, a new burial place for pharaohs was established across the river from Luxor on the west bank of the Nile. No one knows how many Egyptian pharaohs are buried in the Valley of the Kings: new tombs are being discovered all the time. However, the tomb of the boy-king Tutankhamun is undoubtedly the most famous. It is also the most important, because the treasures found inside remained untouched for 3,000 years until the tomb was discovered by the Egyptologist Howard Carter in 1922.

Carvings and Trade

Much of what we know about the Ancient Egyptian civilisation comes from the magnificent carvings that they left behind. The stone used for many of these treasures came from the town of Aswan in the far south of the country.

The Ancient Egyptians were quick to realise that the granite rock found on Aswan's desert plateau was perfect for carving their special statues, obelisks and sculptures. This attractive rock, speckled with pink and black crystals, does not crack easily and polishes to a high sheen. Today, Aswan granite is still highly prized by sculptors, builders and architects.

The granite quarries helped to turn Aswan into a busy trading centre. In Arabic, the name "Aswan" means "market" or "trade". Travellers and camel caravans met here to buy and sell

their precious cargoes of gold, spices and ivory on their way from Africa to Europe and Asia. Aswan still has a reputation for commerce – next to Cairo it has the largest bazaar in Egypt. Successive pharaohs were able to create and maintain one of the ancient world's greatest civilisations. It lasted for more than 3,000 years and still tells its fascinating story today through the treasures they left behind.

What did you think of the guide book?

Extract 1

The pyramids at Giza are one of the world's most visited ancient sites and are a perfect introduction to Ancient Egypt. It is best to arrive early in the morning or towards sunset to experience the true splendour of these three mighty tombs. The pyramids, which tower towards the sky, were built as burial chambers for the pharaohs Khufu, Khafra and Menkaura. They were made from blocks of carefully carved yellow limestone and their corners line up exactly with north, south, east and west. It is hard to imagine that they were built more than 4,500 years ago.

Extract 2

Karnak was the largest temple site ever built by the Ancient Egyptians. For thirteen centuries, each new pharaoh added a new garden or obelisk or altar to mark his time as ruler. But nothing compares with the Great Hypostyle Hall, which was begun by Amenophis and finished many years later by Seti I and his son Ramses. Entering the hall is like walking into a dense stone forest, with row upon row of enormous, spectacularly carved and decorated columns reaching up to the roof.

Koalas

They look like bears, live in trees like monkeys and keep their young in pouches like kangaroos. Koalas are Australia's national symbol and one of nature's most fascinating creatures. Their teddy-bear appearance, soft brown eyes and gentle expression have also made them one of the best loved. Yet, despite their worldwide celebrity and appeal, koalas in the wild are facing the threat of extinction.

Koalas in Crisis

Koalas live in the coastal eucalyptus, or gum, forests of eastern Australia and depend entirely on the trees for their shelter and food. Every year, more than 200,000 acres of Australian forest are cut down to make way for farms and factories, houses and highways, and much of the deforestation takes place along this popular eastern coast. This widespread destruction of such a unique ecosystem has created a habitat crisis for the koalas and forced them into competition with humans for the few remaining areas of natural environment.

The situation is complicated because koalas have special places where they like to forage for food. Within these "home ranges", which can cover up to 200 acres, they follow favourite routes and choose leaves from particular trees. When trees are cut down, or the routes destroyed or built over, koalas quickly become separated from familiar territory and stumble, distressed and disorientated, into human environments.

This has led to an alarming increase in the number of koalas killed in towns and cities, where dangers include traffic, pet dogs, urban foxes and, because koalas are not good swimmers, backyard swimming pools.

Food and Feeding Habits

Koalas are often seen relaxing in their home trees with their eyes closed and their legs dangling over the branches. Many people believe this is because they are "drunk" after eating too much eucalyptus oil. In fact, they adopt this pose because they have a very slow metabolism and need to conserve their energy.

Koalas are nocturnal creatures. They sleep for about 18 hours each day and start their search for food as soon as it gets dark. They live almost entirely on eucalyptus leaves and each night they roam their home ranges along well-known pathways, seeking out exactly the right leaves on the right tree.

Although Australia has more than 600 varieties of eucalyptus, koalas feed from only 140 of them.

Individual koalas often make it even more difficult for themselves by restricting their feeding to just four or five different types. Even then, they choose only the sweetest and juiciest leaves.

Eucalyptus leaves are fibrous, oily, low in nutrients and poisonous to almost every other living creature. Fully-grown adults must chew their way through more than a kilo each night to get as much goodness from them as possible. As the leaves also contain plenty of moisture, koalas seldom have to spend time looking for drinking water.

To digest such a huge meal, and to cope with the harmful toxins, koalas have a particularly strong gut and keep their food in their digestive system for several days. This diet means that all koalas give off a very powerful and distinctive smell of eucalyptus.

Life in the Trees

Early settlers in Australia believed that koalas were monkeys, because they lived high in the trees. Later they were called koala bears, perhaps because of their Latin name *Phascolarctos* (pouched bear) *cinereus* (ash-coloured). They are, in fact, neither monkeys nor bears but tree-dwelling pouched mammals belonging to the marsupial family.

Like all marsupials, koalas carry their young in a pouch. Babies are born after a pregnancy of just 35 days, and are about 1 cm in length (the size of a jelly baby). Without fur, and unable to see or hear, they use their instinct to make their way to the mother's pouch. Here, they attach themselves to the mother and feed on milk for about six months. When the young koalas emerge from the pouch, the mother produces a glutinous liquid which they feed on until their digestive systems are able to cope with the poisons in the eucalyptus leaves.

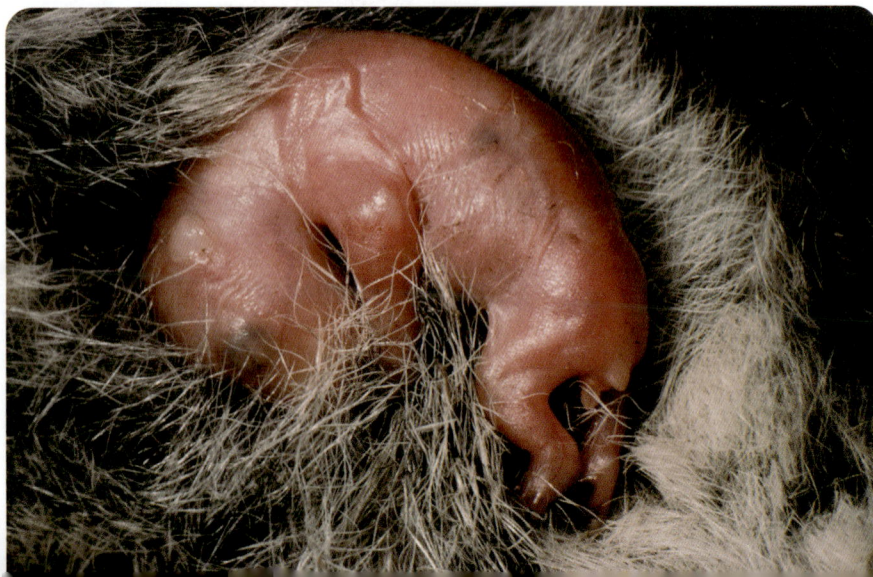

Koalas are a perfect example of how nature adapts creatures to their environment. In order to equip them for life in the trees, koalas have an excellent sense of balance and lean, muscular limbs. Their distinctive front paws, with razor-sharp claws and two thumbs clearly separated from the three fingers, are designed to give them a firm grip as they move through the branches. To climb trees, they leap from the ground, clinging onto the bark tightly with their claws. Then they heave themselves up into the branches. When climbing down, koalas will always descend bottom first. Their thick waterproof fur protects them from all weather conditions – heat, cold and rain – and, to make sitting in trees much more comfortable, koalas have an extra cushion of soft fur around their bottoms.

In Harmony with People

It was when European settlers arrived in Australia that the koalas' problems first began. Before that, koalas had always lived in harmony with their surroundings and with the aboriginal inhabitants. They were hunted for food, even though many tribes believed that they had magic or symbolic powers, but their colonies still grew.

High-quality animal fur was valuable in 19th- and early 20th-century Europe and the USA. Hunters began slaughtering thousands of koalas for profit. In 1927, it was revealed that more than 600,000 koalas were killed in just one month. People were so outraged that the Australian government banned the export of koala fur. But it was too late for the koalas of South Australia. By then they had become extinct.

So what does the future hold for koalas? Today, there are fewer than 100,000 wild koalas, scattered across Queensland, Victoria and New South Wales. Conservation and relocation projects have been set up in these states to try to increase numbers. However, that may not be enough. The continual destruction of Australia's eucalyptus forests is threatening the very future of one of nature's most intriguing and fascinating creatures.

Koalas are now a protected species – but until the eucalyptus forests, on which their lives depend, are also protected, their future remains under serious threat.

Persuasive writing

The Extreme Sports Centre

Looking for an activity holiday with a difference? Look no further – you have found the Extreme Sports Centre! The (safe) centre that offers (safe) extreme sports activities to youngsters aged 7 to 17. (Tell your mum it's safe!)

So, what are extreme sports? Well, anything that's exciting. You can hang glide, bungee and Zorb. You can skate, ski and surf. You can climb, canoe and cave. It's up to you!

**ESCape with ESC.
The Extreme Sports Centre.**

We have various centres around the country that offer extreme sports. All of our centres have comfortable bunk accommodation in cosy log cabins. Guests are expected to make their own beds and look after their cabins. Breakfast is

provided between 7 and 8 a.m. Choose from a continental or cooked version. Continental breakfasts include cereal with fresh milk, newly baked pastries and home-made jams. Cooked breakfasts are made to order with local bread, bacon, sausages and eggs. Packed lunches are supplied as part of the package. These contain a wholesome filled roll, a piece of fruit and a yoghurt. Substantial, tasty meals are provided back at base in the evening.

But – much more important than food – what are you going to try during your activity holiday? Here are just three of the 23 extreme sports that we have on offer. Read these and make your choice.

Log on to our website for details of the other 20 sports and listen to what some children say about us.

Come Zorbing®

It's fast!

It's fun!!

It's for you!!!

Do you fancy trying the latest wacky craze in extreme sports? As long as you are over six years old, you can Zorb – but you do need the oldies to agree to you doing it.

Did you know that the Zorb was invented by two guys from New Zealand? They tried lots of different sizes and ways of making a Zorb and finally came up with a successful one – and believe me, they got it right!

A Zorb weighs 80–90 kilograms and measures 3 metres in height. Basically, it's a big hollow plastic ball inside another bigger hollow plastic ball. The inside ball is attached to the outside ball by thin strands of coloured nylon thread. You slide inside, strap yourself in and then hurtle down a hill at speeds of up to 50 kilometres per hour, cushioned by the air inside the ball. It's unbelievable – the most fantastic feeling in the world!

Here at ESC we have the longest downhill run in the country. As it says on the official website, www.zorb.com, "the Zorb is big, it's fat, it's round and bouncy, you jump inside it, it rolls, you roll too". For added excitement, you can choose to have a bucket of water accompany you on the ride. Can you imagine that?

So, you can try Harness Zorbing – safely strapped in – or you can choose the Washing Machine – you, no harness and a bucket of water or two.

You can Zorb with a friend, you can Zorb alone, it's ab-zorbing!

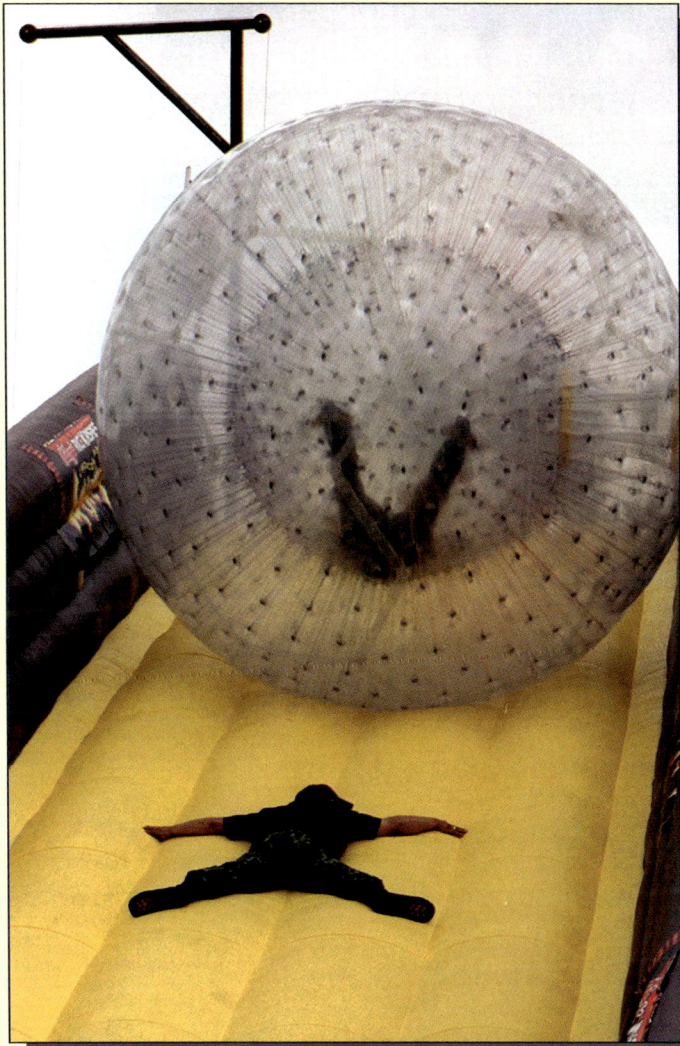

Let's Go Fly a Kite!

We predict that kite surfing is going to be big … really big!

What is it?

Kite surfing is a cross between wind surfing and hang gliding. You ride a surfboard across the sea and are pulled along by a kite.

What do I need?

To kite surf, you need a kite, a board and a wetsuit – not to mention a harness, lines and other technical stuff.

Kite surfing

But we'll supply all of that. You need to supply the nerve!

Is it hard to do?

It's a tricky sport to learn because you need to understand about wind direction and wind speed. But most people find it easier to learn than wind surfing. You may spend your first lesson ploughing up the beach with your nose. However, once you've mastered the art of kite surfing you will soar like a bird above white-capped waves and beautiful beaches. You will wonder why you've never done this before.

How can I practise?

You can have a go on dry land using a skateboard. That gets you used to how it feels and to the way in which the wind behaves. It's also safer than practising in the water as you can easily get pulled out to sea by a strong off-shore wind.

Preparing to kite surf

What will it cost?

Buying kite-surfing equipment is really expensive – kites cost from £400, boards cost from £200. So, the best thing is to give it a try before you buy.

Have a go at kite surfing – it's fantastic – it feels like flying!

Bored? You Won't Be!

Mountain boarding is catching on fast – grab it while you can.

A mountain board is a cross between a skateboard and a snowboard. It can be used on slopes of grass or dirt. The boards are wider than regular skateboards and the wheels stick out at the side. Most boards have bindings to strap your feet into, so that you can do air jumps. Apart from the board itself, you really need a cord to attach the board to you. Just because you've come off and stopped, a board with wheels won't! Padding and a helmet are also a good idea – for reasons that are fairly obvious.

If you have tried any kind of board sport – surfing, snowboarding, skateboarding – you should find mountain boarding both easy to learn and easy to do. And, in this country, what a sensible idea! We don't have enough snow to snowboard, so let's use what we do have – hills.

Here at ESC, we have three downhill runs. The nursery run is for beginners – don't forget the L plates. The blue run is slightly longer and steeper. Then there is the black run – for experts only.

Mountain boarding is one of our most popular extreme sports. It can be done by all ages. If you enjoy the thought of whizzing down a hill with the wind in your hair and the flies in your eyes (and teeth), then mountain boarding is for you.

Rescue Me, I'm a Teacher!

Wanted! Teachers!

The production team at Alternative TV are planning a new reality show and we want the wildest, wackiest, weirdest teachers out there! If you are looking for fame, this could be your big chance to get your face on national TV.

For two weeks, ten teachers will be locked in a real-life, secret-location boarding school with 300 kids. The teachers will be given gruelling and punishing tasks to perform, as well as teaching a full timetable. The kids and the public will judge whether they have been successful.

Cameras will roll 24/7 and the programme will be broadcast at prime time on a daily basis. After the first week, viewers will have the chance to vote out the two teachers they think should be excluded from the school.

The ultimate winner will receive a cash prize for themselves and the chance to audition as a presenter on the next series of "Rescue Me, I'm a Teacher!"

We are looking for a mix of males and females, of all ages. The only rules are that you are a fully qualified teacher and you need to be available for the first two weeks in August.

Auditions will be held over the first two weekends in June. Applicants will be informed of the venues that are closest to their home address. Please apply by letter to the address overleaf. Applications should be received by 31st May.

Letter from Michelle

Dear Alternative TV,

My name is Michelle Thomas. I am 23 years old and have blonde hair and blue eyes. I have been teaching for one year at a primary school in Northdown.

    I would like to apply to be a contestant on "Rescue Me, I'm a Teacher!" I am the ideal contestant because I went to a boarding school, so I know what the life is like. Also, and I'm sure you'll see this as an advantage, I have been on TV before. I once appeared on *Blue Peter* as part of a team of 23 in-line skaters. We did a synchronised dance to a song by Blue. You may remember me, as I fell over during a rather tricky manoeuvre. I am, certainly, the most entertaining person you will find.

    You will be impressed to know that I like putting on a show and therefore think that I could keep the children entertained with my song and dance routines. It wouldn't be very difficult to organise a performance by the pupils in the school, providing I was there for the full two weeks.

Another point in my favour is that my first love is dancing. I would really like to be a dancer. In fact, my headteacher said only the other day that she thought that would be a good career move for me. Actually, the idea of winning and becoming a TV presenter on "Rescue Me, I'm a Teacher!" is very appealing as it would appear that my teaching contract may well end in July.

Finally, I would like to say that my pupils are willing to back up my application to leave my current school and take up a job elsewhere.

Yours faithfully,

Michelle Thomas

Letter from Charli

Hi "Rescue Me, I'm a Teacher!",

I'm a newly qualified teacher and my pupils have suggested that I get in touch with you. They think that I would make a great contestant on "Rescue Me, I'm a Teacher!" because I'm a good sport and they adore the work I give them. They said they would love to be locked up with me for two weeks! In fact, they would like to volunteer to be the kids in the boarding school.

Together, we have prepared a timetable of teaching for a day in the "Rescue Me, I'm a Teacher!" boarding school.

9 – 10	10 – 11	11 – 12	12 – 1	1 – 2	2 – 3
Play "Hunt the Register". Play "Hunt the Pupils".	"Supermarket Sweep" – collecting ingredients for lunch.	"Ready, Steady, Cook" – preparation of lunch using limited ingredients.	Lunchtime – outdoor eating.	Pupils tidy up. Play "Hunt the Teacher".	Teacher gets her own back and children write about the day.

As you can see, this timetable offers a mix of challenges for both the teacher and the children.

Finally, I would like to say a few words about myself. I am very sporty – I play basketball, ladies' football and rugby. I like skateboarding and skiing. So, I think if the challenges in the "Rescue Me, I'm a Teacher!" boarding school were sport-based then I would be a sure-fire winner.

Please – give me a chance!!

Charli "Sporty" Jones

Letter from Mike

6, High Street

Bablington

Midshire

The Producer, "Rescue Me,

I'm a Teacher!"

Alternative TV

Cherrystone Lane

London

WX44 007

Dear Sir,

I noted with interest your recent advert for contestants on the above reality TV show in last week's copy of *Teacher Weekly* and I would like to apply to take part.

I was particularly interested in the gruelling and punishing tasks that the contestants will be given to perform. I think I would be well suited to these challenges as I face them on a daily basis in my current school – which I would prefer not to name.

In the first place, my Year 5 class are constantly playing tricks on me. However, I have managed to carry on teaching despite a recent dose of food poisoning due to an unfortunate incident involving my packed lunch. When they let down the tyres on my car, I soon overcame the problem by supplying four pupils with bicycle pumps and allowing them time to re-inflate the tyres. They then wrote a recount of the event during the Literacy Hour. I think that this provides a good example of carrying on teaching in the face of adversity.

I would like to add that the idea of being locked up is not a problem to me. Only last year, I was stuck in the PE cupboard overnight when Darren James forgot to tell the caretaker that I was in there counting the footballs and goalposts. I certainly feel that the children in the boarding school would benefit from my experiences.

In addition, your comment on searching for male teachers – young or old – is relevant to my application as I certainly fit that description. I have been teaching for ten years and, although I am only 33, I look 50.

I look forward to hearing from you and feel confident that I am the right man for the programme.

Yours faithfully,

Mike Pratt